LEVEL UP

30-DAY GUIDE TO PURSUE YOUR PASSION & BUILD YOUR BRAND TO MAKE A PROFIT!

BY
TIFFANY S. GREENE- MOORER

ispeak
publishing company

Little Rock, Arkansas

Level Up: 30-Day Guide to Pursue Your Passion & Build Your Brand to Make A Profit!

All Scriptures come from the **English Standard, New American Standard, New International Version, Amplified, New Living Translation, King James, American King James** and **New King James** versions of the Holy Bible.

Disclaimer

All the material contained in this book is provided for educational and informational purposes only. No responsibility can be taken for any results or outcomes resulting from the use of this material.

While every attempt has been made to provide information that is both accurate and effective, the author does not assume any responsibility for the accuracy or use/misuse of this information.

Printed in the United States of America

ISpeak Publishing Service
Little Rock, AR.
501-519-6996

The Mentees' Reviews

Sannecia Davis

As kids, we all want to grow up and be lawyers, teachers or doctors; no one ever aspires to be a drug addict. Street life and addiction were issues I battled just about all my life. I was raised in church, so I could never forget what my grandmother instilled in me. I began to pray, believing that God was going to answer my prayers. He did one day. I was invited to a women's conference and that is when I met Ms. Tiffany, who spoke about winning and referenced her book, *I Still Win.* I will never forget the message she brought, as she was speaking my life back into me! When I left that church, my life was forever changed. I draw from *I Still Win* as my daily motivation after beginning the day with prayer. God Bless Ms. Tiffany!

Tahlea Robinson

Pastor Moorer has been more than a great mentor in my life. She has been a great influencer, a confidante, and a spiritual counselor. All the tools I've gained thus far to become a successful author, and to be successful in any future endeavors, have come straight from her own life practices! That's what makes Pastor Moorer so real. She lives by the principles she teaches, which has made it easy for me to follow her lead and adhere to the ministry she puts forth. I would have never been able to publish my first book without her. She is a wonderful life coach and whatever she says is "facts"! She is a boss at what she does!

Christel West

I am so grateful for Tiffany Moorer. Her heart, her passion and her love for people are exhibited through her work. I was two years into trying to complete my book when I signed up to be mentored by Tiffany. I had no idea that she would exceed my expectations by going the extra mile to make sure that I was equipped and that I understood the material provided. Despite my many personal trials, which caused me to have to stop our sessions on several occasions, her support remained consistent ... because of it, what seemed to be impossible became possible. I absolutely love her heart and her passion to see others succeed. When Tiffany read the final edit of my book, she celebrated with me. If you have a story and are not sure which direction to go in, she can lead you, because she has already traveled the road. Tiffany Moorer, I would personally like to say thank you for saying yes to God and obediently walking in your gift and calling. If you had not been in position, I could not have delivered. Thank you!

TABLE OF CONTENTS

Dedication

To my husband, Ernest Moorer,

Thank you for being my Number One fan. No matter what I set out to do, you are always in the stands routing for me and shouting out, "You are awesome!" It is a joy sharing life with you and growing with you in every facet of our relationship. I never thought I could love again, but you have come into my life and shown me what true love really looks like. Thank you, my love!

To my **sons, Dion, Kedric and Terrance**,

Having you all in my life is one of the reasons I strive so hard to be the best I can be! I hope my life is a great example for each of you to live by. You all supported my first book, and now with this book, you each have pushed me to continue my dream of becoming a bestselling author. Thank you all for your continued support and love!

To my bonus daughter, Tahlea Robinson,

Thank you for being the daughter I have always desired to have. I hope the drive for success you see in me is what motivates you to be just as great for my granddaughter, Kynleigh. You have been a great support for my son (your husband), Kynleigh and myself. Thank you for being who you are in our lives. I hope this book inspires you even more to push toward the greatness God has purposed in you!

To Granny Rose, my spiritual advisor and prayer warrior,

Thank you for being a woman of faith, and full of WISDOM! I don't know where I would be without your spiritual guidance. All that I do in life, I do with the hope that I can make you proud of me! There is nothing I will ever do without giving you credit for the wisdom you have given me. You are the epitome of a woman of faith and excellence. Thank you for mentoring me! As I always say, you will always be my Number One "S-HERO"!

To my Mentees,

Thank you for trusting in my guidance and mentorship. I have coached and mentored many of you over the years; you continue to challenge me to be better. Thank you for believing in me!

Last but not least, I thank each of you who will take the advice in this book and use it to change your life for the better. This book was written for you to understand how to Pursue your Passion and, most importantly, Build your Brand to Make a Profit!

ACKNOWLEDGMENTS

I am a firm believer that you can accomplish anything to which you put your mind and heart. Each of us has been purposed to do something on this earth. Whatever your passion is, you are challenged to pursue it. I urge you to live your life in pursuit of happiness and peace, regardless of what you do.

I thank my Changed Life International Ministries family for believing in me and always being one of the biggest supporters of my business ventures. You have been such a supportive team.

I am truly grateful to my husband … the best anyone could ever ask for. Thank you, Ernest Moorer, for pushing and supporting me in every creative idea the Lord leads me to accomplish. You always take a front seat to assist in any way you can. I love you!

I also offer my greatest appreciation to my editor, Helaine R. Williams of Make It Plain Ministries. Thank you for countless hours of providing the best service anyone could ask for. Thank you for your creativity and, most importantly, encouraging me throughout this entire project. You are the BEST!

I am forever thankful to one of my favorite uncles, Victor Greene, for teaching me how to Level Up my finances. You've taught me how to see beyond the right-now to leaving a legacy and inheritance for my family. Your one-on-one coaching has empowered me in ways that are priceless. Thank you for introducing me to a wealthy mindset. I love you!

Lastly, I thank my team of mentees. Thank you for your passion to learn, for trusting me, and for following the steps I have poured into you. I could not coach without having mentees who are hungry for the challenge. You all have Leveled Up because you believed in yourselves! Kudos to you.

Introduction

After spending more than 25 years in the corporate world, working for the State of Arkansas Social Services, I realized I was not fulfilling my purpose. I had a passion and drive for something far more than what I was doing every day. Although I received fulfilment from serving the public, I still felt that something was missing. I always had a desire to start my own business and help others to pursue their dreams.

Making the decision to act on this desire, I read every book I could get my hands on that was related to entrepreneurship and investing. In my research, I discovered that real estate is very lucrative, offering a great return on investment. I connected with someone who had purchased many rental properties and had extensive knowledge in real-estate investing. After researching properties as well as state laws about property investment, I purchased my first rental property with cash in 2014. Was this a new challenge for me? Yes! I had never done this before. But I knew it was the first step to becoming financially secure. I knew it would put me on the road to Leveling Up as a BOSS.

The first house I purchased was a rental-ready, three-bedroom brick home worth far more than what I purchased it for. I paid cash. A year later, I had saved up enough money from the rental income to purchase another rental house … again with cash. This four-bedroom home was another great investment; it, too, was rental ready. Both properties were paid for in full; this increased my assets and proved to be a great BOSS move! I had now learned that each one of these properties would bring enough profit to enable me to purchase a new rental property at least every two years. I was well on my way to becoming a successful entrepreneur.

I had read many books by and about millionaires, many of whom stated that they had multiple streams of income. It was now my desire to branch into other business ventures. I knew I was on to something; it was up to me to make the first step, *to believe in myself*, to achieve what I desired. I knew that whatever I was going to do would be more exciting than clocking into a 9-to-5 job every day. I'd enjoyed hunting for investment property, purchasing it and preparing it to be rented out for profit. Now I was in search of my next passion.

While journaling — something I did daily — I realized that this was something I was passionate about. I loved to write. I'm not the *best* writer, but I loved to express myself in writing. When writing or reading, I found a place of peace and relaxation. *Here's another area in which I can profit from my passion*, I realized. Then I began to research everything I could find concerning writing, editing, publishing and marketing a book. In the spring of 2015, I self-published and released my first book, *I Still Win*, in which I shared my life story of love, tragedy and triumph.

I Still Win propelled me into several additional streams of income. I branded this book as a self-help book and developed ancillary coaching material and products that still bring me great profit today. Not only was the book a great BOSS move, but once I was able to add "author" to my list of business ventures, I was inundated with requests to show others how to become authors. Now that might seem strange, with this being my first book, that I would receive all these requests. But if your book is branded with excellence and written with perfection, its quality will draw an audience. I now had a different *level* of audience, one I'd never anticipated when I wrote my book. What do you think I did with this audience? Yes, I made another BOSS move — I started another business! I created ISpeak Publishing LLC to help other self-publishers see their dreams come true as bestselling authors. ISpeak Publishing was born of my challenging myself to do something I had never done before and believing in myself to become an author. I now coach prospective authors and publish the books they birth. I partnered with a professional editor who perfects my clients' work.

Yes, I have a legitimate professional publishing company that brings in great profit and provides excellent service … again, simply because I challenged myself. Why is this so important? Because you need to know that your passion can work for you, too. Aren't you tired of doing the same thing day in, day out, on a job that's not only unfulfilling but barely gets you from paycheck to paycheck? Let me help you come out of your comfort zone to Pursue your Passion and Define your Purpose! In doing so, you will begin to Build Your Brand and Make a Profit.

Give me 30 days to change your LIFE! This book will help you to create a life of freedom and abundance, doing what you love while making an impact on the world. We are all born with unique sets of gifts, talents and skills. It's time for you to gain crystal clarity of your own unique abilities and fulfill your purpose! Your passion is directly connected to your purpose in life. Each of us has the ability to obtain wealth, which is part of our purpose. YOU have the ability to create an abundant life for yourself! The purpose of this book is to help you, in 30 days, to tap into the wisdom to get that wealth!

A 30-day challenge is a great way to force yourself out of your comfort zone, improve your personal skills and work toward your life's purpose. Why 30 days? Because 30 days is long enough for you to learn some important ways to change your life for the better, but it's also short enough to be manageable. The bottom line: In 30 days, you can make a big difference in your life.

If you do what you love, you'll never work a day in your life.

– Marc Anthony, musician

LET'S GET STARTED!

For the next 30 days, I will be sharing inspirational topics that will build your confidence and fuel your passion to take on the challenge that will Level Up your next BOSS move! Take a minute to think about what life would be like if you were doing what you love to do … and making a profit while doing it.

Maybe you grew up in a working-class home where you watched your parents dutifully put in their shifts at "the plant." They worked Monday through Friday from 7 a.m. to 4 p.m., just so they could enjoy the weekend off and two weeks at the campground (or visiting relatives) each summer.

Perhaps you went off to college and studied law or sales or biology, and now you feel trapped in a job you don't love. You'd like to change course, but what if you make the wrong choice? What else are you even qualified to do? And what about those student loans?

Here's another dilemma for those of you who feel as if you're "working for the weekend" and not pursuing your passion: How can you even *know* what you want to be when you grow up?

Sound familiar?

The truth is, millions of people out there trudge off to work every day, wishing they were anywhere else, and hoping one day to find what really inspires them. If that's you, then rest assured that you are not alone.

But know this, too: There is still time to discover your passion and start doing the work you love.

PASSION

Nothing great in the world has been accomplished without passion.
— **Georg Wilhelm Friedrich Hegel**

Purpose may point you in the right direction but it's passion that propels you.
— **Travis McAshan**

HOW BAD DO YOU WANT IT?

I ran across a Scripture in the Bible that is very interesting. I literally begin to pray over this Scripture, asking God to show me how to apply it to my life.

But remember the LORD your God, for it is he who gives you the ability to produce wealth, and so confirms his covenant, which he swore to your ancestors, as it is today. (Deuteronomy 8:18)

I knew there was more to life than living paycheck to paycheck. This was a part of my faith that I needed to activate in my life. If the Scripture states that the Lord will give me the ability to produce wealth, it was possible that I could do something to produce wealth! If God gives us power to become rich, to become wealthy, to become successful, then He must not be *against* riches, wealth and success. He must *want* us to be rich, wealthy, and successful!

I think most Christians' first take on this Scripture is that it can't mean what it appears to say. The first thought that came to me was, *This must mean* spiritual *wealth and riches* (whatever that means). But, if you look at the rest of the chapter, you'll see that it's referring to literal, "ordinary" wealth and riches. Being wealthy or having success is a part of God's desire for our lives. We must understand that being poor and suffering lack is *not* God's desire for us. However, it is up to us to tap into the wisdom, and the witty inventions, He gives us to produce wealth. This is God's will not just for the children of Israel, but for all of us. *This is the way things are supposed to be.*

When I looked at the "power" or the "ability" part of that promise, I figured it had to be referring to the ability to work hard. That's the power, the ability, God gives us ... life, breath, strength to work hard. I believe what the Scripture says ... that God has given each of us the power and the ability to obtain wealth. That may be as simple as ***physical, mental*** and ***spiritual*** ability to get wealth.

I know there may be some of you who don't understand the spiritual ability to get wealth. But I want to insert another Scripture for you to think on as we dissect ***Deuteronomy 8:18.*** Stick a pin here and think about this promise from God in ***Proverbs 8:12***: *"I, wisdom, dwell with prudence and find out knowledge of witty inventions."* Prudence is the practical application of wisdom. It leads to "witty inventions." In other Bible translations, the phrase "witty inventions" is changed to "discretion," "sound judgment" and "foresight." I believe it is God who gives us wisdom and knowledge of witty inventions ... essential for wealth creation. When we have the mind of Christ, it is He who will lead us to wealth. ***1 Corinthians 2:16*** says, *"For who hath known the mind of the Lord, that he may instruct him? But we have the mind of Christ."* The mind of Christ, with all its potential and potency, is within us. The mind of Christ is full of the wisdom of God and it is by wisdom that everything in this world was created. I believe there is untapped potential within every Christian to create things because of the mind of Christ (that is full of the wisdom of God) within them.

One of the outpourings of God's wisdom is the "knowledge of witty inventions." I know most of us could use more money. I often hear Christians confess **Proverbs 13:22**, which says that the wealth of the wicked is laid up for the just. Could it be that the wealth of the wicked, that is laid up for the just, is to come to us via something we create, like a product or a service? Could it be that while we are waiting for someone to dump money on us, God — through His wisdom and the mind of Christ in us — is giving us new ideas every day, and we're overlooking them? I think the mind of Christ could come up with many things that can solve a problem or satisfy a need: a new song, technology, smartphone app, book, medicine or idea that leads to a product or service.

Now, back to **Deuteronomy 8:18**. The Bible says that if you serve God, He will give you power to become rich. Not power to sub-sist, or get by, or have your basic needs supplied — but power to become rich! Power to have more than enough. Power to be abun-dantly supplied.

This power to become rich is not limited to people who are young and strong and able to work hard. This promise to give power to produce wealth is not limited to people who are born in "good circumstances." This power is available to all — young and old, strong and weak, smart and not so smart. This power to become rich is what God has promised to give. It is what He desires to do for those who worship Him. The question I have for you in this 30-day challenge is **How Bad Do You Want It?**

Deuteronomy 8:18

But remember the LORD your God, for it is he who gives you the ability to produce wealth, and so confirms his covenant, which he swore to your ancestors, as it is today.

You must *believe* you can produce wealth. Take today to reflect and write about the things you are passionate about. Take note of the gifts and talents that God has given you!

_____

_____

_____

_____

_____

_____

_____

_____

_____

_____

_____

_____

BELIEVE YOU CAN DO IT!

S o, you are probably wondering why I haven't tapped into this principle of wealth yet.

I would like to submit to you today that many people are sitting and waiting for something to happen. But nothing will come to you if you don't make the first step to produce. Faith is an action word. If we are going to have what we want, we must not only put *faith* on it, we must put *action* on it. As stated in ***James 2:14:*** "*What good is it, my brothers, if someone says he has faith but does not have works? Can that faith save him?*" If you are going to produce profit … if you're going to be successful in *any* area of your life, matter of fact … you must put work with your faith. We often sit back and dream about having wealth, but we don't put the work in to produce wealth. Or we see it as possible for others, but not for ourselves. Each of us has been given gifts and talents that we can utilize to produce wealth! Many of us overlook those gifts and talents because we don't think they are important; we assume that nobody would be interested in our services. However, that is far from the truth. We are taking advantage of the gifts and talents of others every day! Right at this moment, I'm typing on a computer. Someone worked on their passion and used their gifts and talents to get wealth by developing a computer that is being used in many capacities today. Steve Jobs and Bill Gates became wealthy men because they used their talents and gifts. Jobs emerged with a passion to develop Apple computers; Gates, with a passion to develop Microsoft software. They built multibillion-dollar corporations simply because they used their power to produce wealth.

The question I have for you today is: Where is your faith? We can't apply the wealth Scriptures to our lives if we lack faith. Why ask God for something you don't believe you can obtain? Every successful person stepped out on passion and faith to become successful. You don't become successful without taking a risk. Of course, you're going to fail here and there. That's all a part of growing. But you will never succeed if you are fearful of taking the leap.

Another Scripture that helped me become successful is **_Jeremiah 17:7-8:_** _"But blessed are those who trust in the Lord and have made the Lord their hope and confidence. They are like trees planted along a riverbank, with roots that reach deep into the water. Such trees are not bothered by the heat or worried by long months of drought. Their leaves stay green, and they never stop producing fruit."_

Every business venture I started was done so in faith. I had to believe I could achieve whatever I put my mind to. I also had to trust God. This Scripture was reassurance that if I was going to be blessed, I had to do so! My confidence could not be in man — in what others thought about me. I was confident that the Lord would open doors for me to walk into; doors that others did not see. You must do the same thing as an entrepreneur. You must believe you can walk into the boardroom and confidently pitch your business to anybody on any level. The illustration of the trees in this Scripture is powerful in that the trees are planted by a riverbank, with roots that reach deep into the ground and access the water that gives them their sustenance. In other words, my faith must be deep in the Lord to understand the principles of wealth. Then, when famine or hard times arise, I am not moved! My abundance of wealth is so preserved that in times of market trouble, or if the economy fails, my fruit will continue to produce. That's what the Scripture means when it says the trees' leaves will stay green, and they will never stop producing fruit.

You can't be afraid to step out in faith to start your business, to write your book, to patent your invention, to establish your school. Wherever your passion and purpose lead you, remember that God has already given you the provision; you just need to activate your faith to reach your blessed place!

Jeremiah 17:7-8

But blessed are those who trust in the Lord and have made the Lord their hope and confidence. They are like trees planted along a riverbank, with roots that reach deep into the water. Such trees are not bothered by the heat or worried by long months of drought. Their leaves stay green, and they never stop producing fruit.

What are the fears holding you back today from starting your own business, writing the book or doing what you are most passionate about doing?

_____

_____

_____

_____

_____

_____

_____

_____

_____

_____

_____

UNLOCK YOUR PASSION

What does purpose have to do with passion? Many people don't understand that their passion is directly connected to their purpose. The thing you are passionate about in life is oftentimes the very thing God has purposed and gifted you to do on earth. The Scripture says in *Ephesians 11:1:* *"In Him also we have received an inheritance [a destiny — we were claimed by God as His own], having been predestined (chosen, appointed beforehand) according to the purpose of Him who works everything in agreement with the counsel and design of His will."* It is our purpose that drives our passion, and it comes from the Lord. It is what He calls an inheritance.

Now when I speak of an inheritance, I am referring to something that will make me better, not worse. It is something that is to bring me to greater, not to lack. The Lord's purpose is to bring us to a greater understanding of His inheritance for us. Not only that, but the Scripture says we were *chosen* for it … appointed beforehand. Therefore, there is something within me that I have inherited from the Lord to do in the earth. I was called to do it! I was chosen to do it! This is where my passion comes from. God is calling us to prosper as our souls prosper.

When we can understand our purpose, and the inheritance God has given us in the earth as His children, we can better understand His plan of wealth and prosperity for our lives. I love the ending of this Scripture. It says, *"according to the purpose of Him who works every-thing in agreement with the counsel and design of His will."* I told you earlier in this book that it is God's will for us to live a life of abundance and wealth. It is not His will for us to live in lack! He will work everything in agreement with the counsel and design (purpose) He has for our lives. We get caught up in *our* plans and not *His* plans, which is why we seem to get lost along the way and find ourselves in dead-end jobs, dead-end situations and unfulfilled patterns in life. All these plans we have in our hearts won't work if they don't line up with His will for our lives. Consider **Proverbs 19:21:** *"Many are the plans in a person's heart, but it is the Lord's purpose that prevails."*

Think about the Apostle Paul and all he accomplished in two decades of ministry. What made him tick? What drove him to carry out the work that he did? In **Philippians 3:7-9,** he says that *"whatever was to my profit I now consider loss for the sake of Christ. What is more, I consider everything a loss compared to the surpassing greatness of knowing Christ Jesus my Lord, for whose sake I have lost all things. I consider them rubbish, that I may gain Christ and be found in him, not having a righteousness of my own that comes from the law, but that which is through faith in Christ – the righteousness that comes from God and is by faith."*

This passage explodes with Paul's passion for his calling! Effective leaders like Paul are those who have figured out what they stand for. They have identified their purpose and pursue it with a passion.

Before his dramatic conversion in the ninth chapter of Acts, Paul followed a different purpose in life. As a Pharisee, Paul had attained the highest levels of status. In this instance, he could have boasted about his religious training, heritage and practice. He had been, in every sense, a "Hebrew of Hebrews," and his credentials would have impressed the most devoted Jew. He was a passionate man, but in his old life he was passionate about the wrong things. After his encounter with the risen Lord, Paul considered all he had attained through religious effort to be garbage when compared with the value of knowing Christ. Paul was more than happy to throw away all he had attained to know Christ.

Paul preached that in Christ, he and all believers possess all the righteousness of God. We can have peace with the One who created us, the One for whom we were made. Because of the infinite *worth* of knowing Christ, Paul devoted his life to knowing the Savior. That was his purpose and his passion. That purpose and that passion shaped all he did and influenced all he led. Paul is the most passionate Biblical character I can think of to illustrate how our passion should lead to our purpose. Although Paul's path may be very different from your purpose, the *idea* of his passion is what you want to search for.

What is your purpose? I am willing to believe your purpose is merged with your passion. I want to challenge you to search your heart for purpose. Not desires. Not plans that others have tried to put on your life. What is your *purpose*? I know it may seem difficult to identify, but when you think of what you are currently passionate about, you'll see that this is where your purpose lies. There are some people who are gifted to sing, write, speak, inspire, administrate. What is that thing you have already been doing, that thing you love to do, but don't see as an avenue for profit?

Ephesians 11:1

In Him also we have received an inheritance [a destiny — we were claimed by God as His own], having been predestined (chosen, appointed beforehand) according to the purpose of Him who works everything in agreement with the counsel and design of His will.

Take time to write about your passion and purpose. Identify your passions-with-profit ideas!

_____

_____

_____

_____

_____

_____

_____

_____

_____

_____

_____

_____

_____

MASTER MIND

Many of us know what we are passionate about. Many of us even know what we are purposed to do in the earth. The struggle comes in how to execute what we have a passion to do. In other words, we have failed to consider our fields.

I am reminded of the Scripture that is often noted as the Proverbs 31 "Virtuous Woman" Scripture. The actions of the Virtuous Woman are completely applicable today. **Proverbs 31:16** shows us that *"she considereth a field, and buyeth it: with the fruit of her hands she planteth a vineyard."* This woman thought of a **Master Plan**. She didn't wait for someone to advise her on how to bring wealth to her house. She considered a field, bought it and put her hands to work. This let me know that the woman had *skills*. She knew what to do and she only needed to consider what field she would use to bring about her wealth! Beyond that, she's savvy. She's not only educated about the world in general; she's educated about the world of business in particular … and she's not afraid to interact with that world, whether it be as a merchant or a buyer. She knows how to use her skills to provide for her family. She knows how to use her strengths to her best advantage, and she fully realizes how valuable her efforts are.

The Virtuous Woman doesn't buy the property just because it's cute; she buys it because she has a master plan to produce wealth.

She is going to plant and work the field. Once the field yields a harvest and becomes profitable, she can upgrade to a vineyard, which will gain her family entry into the lucrative wine market. This isn't a vanity purchase. It is an investment in her family's future ... an investment into which she puts time, labor and her perseverance. With such commitment, investments will appreciate and pay off. No doubt this Virtuous Woman is a female entrepreneur!

You, too, must have a master plan. If you would begin to consider what knowledge, skills and talents you already possess, you, too, can consider your field and bring wealth to your household.

Proverbs 31:16-18

She considers a field and buys it; From her profits she plants a vineyard. She girds herself with strength, And strengthens her arms. She perceives that her merchandise is good, And her lamp does not go out by night …

Write down your business goals.

_____

_____

_____

_____

_____

_____

_____

_____

_____

_____

_____

_____

_____

_____

LEAP OF FAITH

N otice that the Virtuous Woman made an investment first. Most of us are afraid to make investments, but for this woman to make a profit, she had to take the leap of faith and make an investment to purchase the field. She was not afraid to invest in what she was expecting: a return. You can't bring wealth without an investment! This book is an investment for you to begin to think about how to devise your plan for wealth.

Also notice that in the Scripture, the Virtuous Woman used her hands to plant a vineyard. If you are going to succeed in business, you must put in the work! Nothing worthwhile will come to you easily. If something comes to you easily, trust me — it will not last. This woman put in the work to plant seed in the ground, then she stepped back and waited for the harvest to come. You can't be afraid to take the leap of faith, to put in the work. Successful entrepreneurship and wealth gain will not happen overnight; this is not a get-rich-quick scheme. In addition to a well-thought-out plan, in addition to investment, wealth gain takes *time*. Sam Walton, Bill Gates and Oprah Winfrey didn't become billionaires overnight. However, they each "considered a field," took a leap of faith and emerged with wealth!

I know you are probably wondering, "How do I get started on my plan for wealth?" If you are ready to take this journey, I say again that you must be prepared for work! Proverbs 31:18 reveals this about the Virtuous Woman: *"her candle goeth not out by night,"* meaning that she was up late at night, working. This woman understood that if wealth was going to come to her house, she could not play around. She made use of all the time she had … even late at night, while everyone else in the house was asleep. Why is this important? Most of the time I put in as a budding entrepreneur was late at night; I was still doing my 9-to-5 job in the daytime. If you are like most people, you are still on *your* 9-to-5 job, trying to see your way out of the hustle and bustle of life. If you're going to be successful, you must make use of ALL your time and take the Leap to Wealth!

Proverbs 6:6 –11

Take a lesson from the ants, your lazybones. Learn from their ways and become wise! Though they have no prince or governor or ruler to make them work, they labor hard all summer, gathering food for the winter. But you, lazybones, how long will you sleep? When will you wake up? A little extra sleep, a little more slumber, a little folding of the hands to rest — then poverty will pounce on you like a bandit; scarcity will attack you like an armed robber.

Write down the work you believe you must do to solidify your "leap of faith" into entrepreneurship.

_____

_____

_____

_____

_____

_____

_____

_____

_____

_____

THE TIME IS NOW!

Consider the life cycle of a seed. First, it must be planted. Once it's planted, the seed grows. Growth takes time.

Therefore, it can be helpful to remember this principle as "seed, time, and then harvest." Seed, time and harvest are the three phases of receiving what God has provided for you. First, you plant the seed. Then you must exercise patience, and keep believing, while the seed grows. Finally, you will reap a harvest of blessing.

The "time" phase can be the toughest part of the process. Did you know that time is valuable? It is, and any successful person understands the importance of maximizing it. Pursuing your passion and building your brand for profit takes *mastering your time*! "Why is time so important?" you may be asking. If you do not understand the value of time, especially in conjunction with planning, you most likely will *not* be successful in business. The saying goes that if a man doesn't plan, then he plans to fail. The Bible also speaks of the danger of being unprepared, which simply means failing to set goals. And I know I am a better businesswoman when I set a plan and then maximize my time to execute it. If you allow the principle of seed, time and harvest to work in your life, you will have financial abundance.

And that brings me to goal setting. Goals are a very important part of anyone's life. Especially if you are starting a new business venture, setting and pursuing a goal is a vital part of your success. Setting goals is simply managing time! If you planted that seed and understand that the growth of that seed will take time, you will realize this does not mean giving up the next day, when you don't see what you are expecting. You must have faith that the seed will break out of the soil and grow. God's law of seed, time and harvest guarantees us that the seed will grow if we give it *water* and *time*. The same is true with investing in your business. Many people with God-given dreams of succeeding in business fall by the wayside because they want their prosperity *right now*. Don't be one of them. Don't give up if you have a bad day, or if you have not met your goals as soon as you'd hoped you would. Give your investments time to grow.

Genesis 8:22

As long as the earth endures, seedtime and harvest, cold and heat, summer and winter, day and night will never cease.

Take time to write your business goals!

_____

_____

_____

_____

_____

_____

_____

_____

_____

_____

_____

_____

_____

_____

_____

_____

SETTING BUSINESS GOALS

Every small-business owner knows that if you're not having fun and enjoying your work, it's tough to stay motivated. And if you're not feeling motivated, it's nearly impossible to grow.

People who live their lives without goals often fail to achieve what they could have achieved. Some people have this philosophy of being content all the time. Contentment is good to some extent; the Apostle Paul writes in Philippians 4:11 that *"I have learned to be content whatever the circumstances"* (New Living Translation). But that attitude does not work in the long run when it comes to entrepreneurship. You always need some type of structure to help motivate you to move on; this structure comes in the form of setting goals. Goal setting, and achieving goals, call for a thorough planning process. This process starts with identifying goals in the first place; breaking them down into smaller, achievable steps; then acting toward them.

What Are Goals? Goals are fundamental keys to success and achievement. This definition may sound a little confusing, but you need to understand that goals give you the meaning of life. Without goals, you just live your life, but *with* goals, you can live your life *with purpose*. Goals help you to centralize your energy. You cannot identify yourself without proper goals in your life. These goals also give you an opportunity to express yourself to others. Without goals, your life is an empty field. Goals make this field colorful and provide meaning to your life.

How to Set your goals

Specify: Be specific with your goal — what your business is about; why it is important to you.

Plan: What are your monthly, six-month, one-year and five-year goals for the business? Break these goals down. Start with your lifetime goals and continue down to your monthly goals … and plan each step to these goals.

Take Action: What actions do you need to take to achieve these goals? Write a to-do list for each goal.

Create: Visualize your goals. Create vision boards and affirmations.

Evaluate: Evaluate each goal regularly and make needed adjustments.

Don't let this list fool you. While these steps appear very easy, they're the core of successful goal achievement — particularly when it comes to bigger goals, for which the whats and hows of accomplishment become more subtle.

People often concentrate on material goals and want to quickly set a target to achieve them. But in my point of view, goal setting should be much broader than that. I will demonstrate the whole process of identifying and pursuing those goals. People often confuse goals with resolutions, but goals are different from resolutions. Resolutions are simply a wakeup call in your life, while goals actually improve your life. If you take your goals seriously, I am

100 percent sure that they will not only make your life more pro-
gressive, they will also help you resolve your problems more easily.

Before you can set goals or achieve anything in your business or
your life, you must understand what really drives you. What is it
that truly gets you up in the morning when all you want to do is
roll over and go back to sleep? What forces you to pick up the
phone to call yet another potential client? What keeps you going,
even when you want to give up? Once you know what drives you,
every decision becomes easier. So, before you start setting goals,
let's spend some time thinking about why you do what you do.

Proverbs 21:5

The plans of the diligent lead to profit as surely as haste leads to poverty.

MONTHLY GOALS	6 MONTHS GOALS	1 YEAR GOALS	5 YEARS GOALS

BUILDING A BUSINESS PLAN

L et me give you three words of advice here: ***Specify your business***! We must be specific about what we plan to do as entrepreneurs. If you are going to be successful, you can't be uncertain about what you plan to do. Being specific about your business plan is important for you and those you will be asking to assist you in this development plan. If you are unsure of where you are going, it will be hard to get someone else to support your plan.

"Then the LORD *answered me and said: 'Write the vision and make it plain on tablets, that he may run who reads it.'"* This principle of the Bible, found in ***Habakkuk 2:2,*** is related to *every* area of our lives, not just in the church. When you write the vision — plan it and make it plain — it is easier not just for you to be guided by what is written, but also for those you would want to partner with. This is necessary even for something as simple as a bank loan application. If you are expecting a bank to back your business with a loan, you will be required to supply a business plan. Oftentimes, a business fails because of the lack of a well-thought-out business plan.

You are probably wondering, *What does a business plan look like?* If so, I am glad you are wondering. A business plan is one of the very first things you should develop before you start your business. This process will take some time, but it is necessary. If you are unsure of how to start, one of the best things you can do is go to your local Small Business Association (SBA) center to ask for free assistance, or build your business plan online at https://www.sba.gov/tools/business-plan/. Your local bank may even offer a class for business- plan writing.

I will offer a short outline (below) of what a business plan should include. You can brainstorm and have strategy meetings with your team, if you have assembled one, to develop a business plan based on this simple model.

Habakkuk 2:2

Then the LORD answered me and said: "Write the vision and make it plain on tablets, That he may run who reads it."

Write out your strategy to establish your business.

_____

_____

_____

_____

_____

_____

_____

_____

_____

_____

_____

_____

_____

_____

_____

_____

_____

DAY 9

MAKING YOUR BUSINESS PLAN COMPELLING

W hat will be different about *your* business plan? Why should any bank consider giving *you* a business loan? How will *your* business benefit the market, the target demographics, the investors? These are some of the questions you need to consider when writing your business plan.

Here are some things you should include in that plan.

A concise but positive description of your company, including objectives and accomplishments. For example, if your company is established, consider describing what it set out to do; the goals it has accomplished to date and how those goals were accomplished; and what lies ahead. If your company is new, summarize what you intend to do; how and when you intend to do it; and how you think you can overcome major obstacles (such as competition).

The legal structure of your business. Indicate whether your business is a sole proprietorship, partnership or corporation (more about this later). If appropriate, define the business type (manufacturing, merchandizing, or service).

Marketing data. Marketing is very important in outlining a compelling business plan. If you believe you have something that's

31

new, innovative or not generally available to the public, *how do you know* that there is a market for it — that people are willing to pay for what you have to offer? (We will talk about marketing in detail on another day.)

An explanation of how you expect to make your business profit-able, based on the products or services you intend to offer, and the time period within which you expect to do so. Once you are ready to open your business, you will need an operating budget to help prioritize expenses. It should include the money you need to survive the first three to six months of operation. Indicate how you intend to control the finances of your company.

Now that you have described the important elements of your business, you may want to **summarize your strategy for their implementation**. If your business is new, prioritize the steps you must take to open your doors for business. Describe your objectives, how you intend to reach them, and the time parameters in which you intend to reach them. If writing a business plan is new for you, check with your local small-business association for free business-writing opportunities.

Proverbs 16:3

Commit to the Lord whatever you do,and he will establish your plans.

Write an outline of the services or products your business will offer.

_____

_____

_____

_____

_____

_____

_____

_____

_____

_____

_____

_____

_____

_____

A BUILDING PLAN FOR INVESTORS

Astrong business plan represents focus. It should show short-term operations with long-term strategy and should encourage efficiency within the business. It helps the business owner to communicate his or her vision to those outside the business and can be crucial for outlining a strong plan to interest investors. Not only is a compelling business plan useful for those outside of the company; it also gives clear direction for those who decide to partner within the company.

Building on the information from Day 9, let's look at some *specifics* for a compelling business plan. First and foremost, any business owner who plans to succeed must clearly identify the service(s) or product(s) offered, the customers who will buy/pay for them, and the competition. As stated in Day 9, a compelling business plan must identify the market. As the business owner, you should know your customers. And in your business plan, you must be able to demonstrate why they need to buy from you. Again, what will make *your* business more attractive to patronize than the businesses similar to yours? This may require you partnering with someone who has a better understanding of the market with which you are trying to interact. *This will require some humility on your part;* however, it will pay off for you in the end. When building a business plan, acquiring insights from market insiders can shave off years of trial and error.

Whatever you do, take your time. Include in your plan all the information that is vital for your business projection. Instead of treating your business plan as a mere document, see it as an *actionable plan* for your business. The real key is demonstrating an understanding of your business that will enable you to talk about it in any level of detail. Think about your business plan being developed in such a way that you can expand or break it down for whatever audience to which you are attempting to appeal. Write your business plan for prospective or current investors, the board, the management team or perhaps just for yourself. Remember: If you can't easily express your vision for your business, you will struggle to raise money from investors … you will struggle to convince prospective employees to join you … and you will struggle to sell to customers, no matter how great your business concept.

As also indicated earlier, a fundamental element of running a successful business is having a firm grip of its finances. When writing a business plan, you'll need detailed financial projections that you know inside out. When providing forecasting data in your plan, make sure it extends to 30, 60 and 90 days, as well as 12 months, three years and five years, to help you understand and set targets for the immediate as well as the long-term future. When writing your plan for investors, remember that the bottom line matters more than most of what you have to say about your business. The investors' priority is the return they will get on their money, so be realistic in telling them what return they can expect.

Your business plan should be revisited at least once a year. One of the key points to remember in writing your compelling business plan is to think about later using this plan as a mental exercise to plan realistically for your future and demonstrate that you and your team have the vision to drive the ship.

Proverbs 24:27

Do your planning and prepare your fields
before building your house.

Look over the business plan you wrote out based on the form in
Day 8 and expound on it according to the points covered in Days
9 and 10.

Building A Team

Building a small-business team is never as easy as it sounds. When you first got started, you probably thought a *lot* about your customers and their needs — and how you could help them. If you are going to be successful at helping them, you must consider building a TEAM! This is not about simply hiring people to complete a task in your business. It's about strategically selecting the right people to join your team. Keeping your business success in mind, you must skillfully select your team.

Building this team will require more than just looking for the most talented people. It's not hard to find talented and skilled people to complete a task. You will need to consider a few other concepts when building your team if you want your business to be successful. If you want to build a strong team:

- Build with people who agree and support your overall business mission/purpose.

- Build with people who will work well together.

- Build with people who will work your vision with commitment.

- Build with people who understand the importance of physically coming together in formal group meetings for open discussion of broad-based issues.

- Build with people who encourage positive, informal interactions among group members.

- Build with people who will instill a "winning" attitude throughout the organization.

- Build with a diverse group of people who can bring multiple perspectives and viewpoints together in a productive manner.

- Build with people who will identify those who might attempt to reverse team-building with jealousy, cynicism or defensive behavior.

When you build a team for your business, you want to build a WINNING team! To build a winning team, you need to not only show people what direction the company is headed in, but also get them to "buy into" this direction. You can't expect people to support your business if they don't agree with where it's headed or, worse, don't even *know* where it's headed.

Specifically, you need to show people:

- Your vision for the future
- Your strategy for getting there
- Why this is the best strategy
- Milestones that mark progress toward company goals

This is not a onetime discussion or announcement. You need to constantly remind people of what the organization stands for … and remind them that it indeed holds a bright future for them.

Now you're off to building a successful team for your business!

Ecclesiastes 4:9

Two are better than one; because they have a good return for their labor:

Consider and write down the types of team members you need for your business, based on job descriptions.

PLAN

You were born to win, but to be a winner, you must plan to win, prepare to win, and expect to win.
— **Zig Ziglar**

It takes as much energy to wish as it does to plan.
— **Eleanor Roosevelt**

THE IMPORTANCE OF STRATEGIC PLANNING

Strategic planning is important to an organization because it provides a sense of direction and outlines measurable goals. Strategic planning is a tool that is useful for guiding day-to-day decisions. It's also useful for evaluating progress and changing approaches when moving forward. In order to make the most of strategic planning, your company should give careful thought to the strategic objectives it outlines, and then back up these objectives with realistic, thoroughly researched, quantifiable benchmarks for evaluating results.

The very first strategic planning most businesses do is in the form of business-plan creation. When you first start your business, you will likely have prepared a mission statement, a budget, and a marketing and promotion plan. The business plan is a good first step, but it needs to be reviewed and updated as the business continues and grows. Long-term strategic objectives help you think in terms of big-picture goals and overarching visions. Align the short-term objectives in your strategic plan with your longer-term goals.

Strategic planning is an important tool for bringing your team together and motivating its members to work with a goal in mind. If your team knows the company's short- and long-term goals, it's easier to stay on task and refocus projects and individuals when they're veering off-track. Strategic objectives provide a shared sense of purpose, a shared dialogue to gauge progress. They also provide milestones to celebrate, once they have been achieved.

Planning out the future of your business through strategic planning is the best way to ensure success. It may seem awkward and difficult at first, but with practice, you will be able to move your business in the right direction.

Proverbs 16:9

In their hearts humans plan their course, but the LORD establishes their steps.

Create a short-term and a long-term outline for your business.

_____

_____

_____

_____

_____

_____

_____

_____

_____

_____

_____

_____

_____

_____

_____

THE LEGAL STRUCTURE OF YOUR BUSINESS

When opening a small business, you should first search and apply for licenses, permits or identification numbers that correspond with the type of service you are offering. Taxes that are commonly applied to businesses include withholding tax, sales and use tax, and unemployment insurance tax. You would need to establish the legal affirmation of your business before visiting your city, county or state revenue office to register it.

Here are a few business-entity structures for you to consider. If you live in Arkansas, forms for some of these entities can be filed online at the Arkansas Secretary of State website.

Sole Proprietorship

A business with a single owner, and no formal or separate form of business structure, is known as a sole proprietorship. The owner has sole control of, and responsibility for, the business. A sole proprietorship is easily formed, allows important decisions to be made quickly, and typically has fewer legal restrictions. In this situation, the owner and the business are indistinguishable. The business has limited life and cannot be transferred (as an entity) to others. Generally, paperwork for sole proprietorships is NOT filed with the

Secretary of State; some is filed at the county level. The sole proprietor's responsibilities include, but are not limited to:

- *Obtaining all capital*
- *Incurring personal liability for all debts and claims against the business*
- *Claiming all profits and losses on the owner's personal income tax return*
- *Obtaining state and local business licenses and permits*

Partnership

A partnership is an association of two or more persons acting as co-owners of a business. A written agreement between the parties involved is highly recommended. This agreement should set out the responsibilities and obligations of the partners, as well as the percentage of ownership. There are several types of partnership:

1. General Partnership

Those involved in a general partnership are not required to file official registration beyond that

required for a sole proprietorship, but they may choose to file with the Secretary

of State's office in order for the business to be on record as a general partnership. Check with

your advisors.

General partnerships:

- *Do not protect the personal assets of the business partners from claims against the partnership*

- *Require the principals to file informational returns with the Internal Revenue Service and local state revenue office*

- *Require partners to share their profits and losses among themselves via establishment of ownership percentage or other legal means. Partners are then required to claim this income or loss on their personal income tax return*

- *Require recording the name of the business with the local/county clerk*

2. Limited Liability Company

A limited liability company (also known as an LLC) is a flexible form of enterprise that blends elements of partnership and corporate structures. It is a legal form of company that provides limited liability to its owners in the vast majority of United States jurisdictions.

The "owners" of an LLC are referred to as "members." Depending on the state, the members can consist of a single individual (one owner), two or more individuals, corporations, other LLCs and even other entities.

Unlike shareholders in a corporation, LLCs are not taxed as a separate business entity. Instead, all profits and losses are "passed through" the business to each member of the LLC. LLC members report profits and losses on their personal federal tax returns, just like the owners of a partnership would.

3. Other

Other legal business entities include corporations, nonprofits, and cooperatives.

If you are unsure which business structure is best for your business, seek advice from a lawyer who specializes in business structures.

Proverbs 21:3

To do what is right and just is more acceptable to the LORD than sacrifice.

Take time to consider, and write down, the legal affirmation of your business.

_____

_____

_____

_____

_____

_____

_____

_____

_____

_____

_____

_____

_____

_____

TAX PREPARATION FOR YOUR BUSINESS

As an entrepreneur, you want to make sure you are adhering to state and federal laws with your business. Never operate a business without first finding out the appropriate steps to take to legally establish it based on your state regulations. If you are unsure of what your state requires, you can review the website of your state revenue office for business registration. You can also contact your local Small Business Association to receive free information on how to establish your business, based on state and federal regulations. In addition, it is a good rule of thumb to speak with an accountant who can assist you in acquiring and maintaining the documents your business will need for tax purposes.

Business registration essentially encompasses a four-step process and applies to all businesses — whether you identify as a freelancer, owner of a home-based or online business, or a franchise owner, regardless of whether or not you are incorporated. Here, according to information from the U.S. Small Business Administration, are a few steps you want to consider when making sure you are following tax laws.

1. ***Register Your "Doing Business As" Name***: This is a fictitious name, assumed name or trade name, and is usually referred to as "DBA." It is different from your personal name, the names of your partners, or the officially registered name of your LLC or corporation. An example is John Doe's sole proprietorship, doing business as "Doe's Lawn Mowing Service." Registering your DBA is done either with your county clerk's office or with your state government, depending on where your business is located. There are a few states that do not require the registering of fictitious business names.

2. ***Register for a Tax Identification Number from the IRS***: Most entrepreneurs use their own social security numbers to pay business taxes. However, if you have employees, you'll also need to apply for an Employer Identification Number (EIN). Employers with employees, business partnerships, corporations and other types of organizations must apply for an EIN Online.

3. ***Register for State and Local Tax Purposes:*** State taxes include income tax, sales tax and unemployment insurance tax (for employers only), while local authorities such as your city or county government oversee business property tax, permits, and licenses. Are you selling products? If you plan to sell products and you are required to collect sales tax, you may need a sales tax permit or vendor's license from your state or local government (or both). To register your business with your state tax agency, and to understand what you need to do based on your business type, visit your state website. Similarly, to register your business

with your city or county tax department, visit your city or county website.

4. ***Register for Permits and Licenses***: These vary by business type and location, but every business needs a basic operating license or permit — even if you are home-based. Most of these permits and licenses come from your local or state government. If your business is involved in activities supervised and regulated by a federal agency — such as selling alcohol, firearms, commercial fishing, etc. — then you may need to obtain a federal license or permit.

Proverbs 21:5

Good planning and hard work lead to prosperity, but hasty shortcuts lead to poverty.

Review your state, federal and county requirements for your business.

MANAGEMENT AND ORGANIZATION

Proper management and organization are vital to your business plan. These will ensure that you are in as much control as possible of what happens with your business and the direction in which it moves. What planning methods will you utilize? If you haven't considered how your business will be structured and managed from day to day, now is the time. Such consideration is very important to your success.

You may have the passion and experience to provide the service or product you are selling, but that may not be enough to keep the business alive. Do you have a need to employ others who have experience in vital areas that you lack? It is important to identify your areas of weakness so that you can partner with those who may be more skilled than you in those areas, or who have the background and experience to help you to make your business a success. In that vein, you need to clearly define the areas of the business that you will personally manage and the areas you will delegate to other managers.

Often, new businesses fail because of lack of organization and poor management. Customers are looking for two things: a five-star product and five-star service. If your business is lacking in either area, it will become one of those businesses that doesn't make it. Proper management is vital to success in both areas. That's why having the right people on your team to execute your mission is very important!

Later in the book, we will discuss business integrity — because the lack of it is one of the main things that will destroy a business before it reaches its full potential.

Meanwhile, here are a few pointers for providing quality service for your customers.

1. *Properly Plan*
2. *Be Responsive*
3. *Anticipate Your Customers' Needs*
4. *Be Honest; Be Transparent*
5. *Be a Part of the Solution*

Following is a company organization template and an organizational/managerial planning guide.

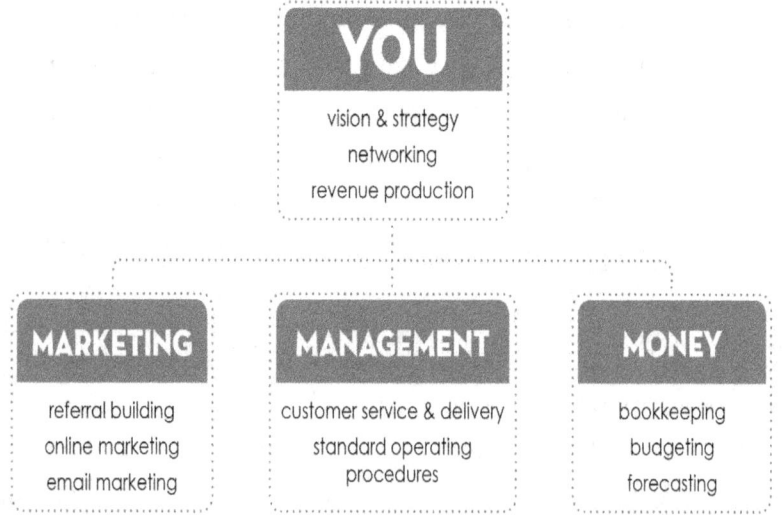

Executive Summary

Write this last so that you can summarize the most important points from your business plan.

Company Ownership/Legal Entity

Sole proprietorship, corporation (type), or partnership

Market Analysis

What is your target market? (Who is most likely to buy your products or use your services?) What are the demographics? What is the size of your potential customer base?

Where are they? How are you going to let them know who and where you are and what you have to offer?

If you believe you have something new, innovative or that isn't generally available: How do you know there is a market for it — that people are willing to pay for what you have to offer?

Consider the market you are trying to reach: Is it growing, shrinking or static?

What percentage of the market do you think you will be able to reach? How will you be able to grow your market share?

Note: You might include a chart to demonstrate key points about your market potential at-a-glance.

Marketing

How well you market your business can play an important role in its success or failure. It is vital to know as much about your potential customers as possible—who they are, what they want (and don't want), and expectations they may have.

Advertising and Promotion

How do you intend to advertise your business?

Which of the following advertising and promotion options offer you the best chances of successfully growing your business: Directory services, social networking websites, media (newspaper, magazine, television, radio), direct mail, telephone solicitation, seminars and other events, joint advertising with other companies, sales representatives, word-of-mouth, other?

How will you determine your advertising budget?

How will you track the results of your advertising and promotion efforts?

CONSIDER THE COST: FINANCIAL RESPONSIBILITY

The way company finances are managed can be the difference between success and failure. Start-up needs should include any one-time-only purchases, such as major equipment or supplies, down payments or deposits, as well as legal and professional fees, licenses/permits, insurance, renovation/design/decoration of your location, personnel costs prior to opening, and advertising or promotion.

Once you are ready to open your business, you will need an operating budget to help prioritize expenses. It should include the money you need to survive the first three to six months of operation and indicate how you intend to control the finances of your company. Include the following expenses: rent, utilities, insurance, payroll (including taxes), loan payments, office supplies, travel and entertainment, legal and accounting, advertising and promotion, repairs and maintenance, depreciation, and any other categories specific to your business.

Now that you know what you want your business and your life to look like — and more importantly, *why* you want it to look like that — it's time to set some financial goals. When setting your goals, keep the S.M.A.R.T. model in mind. Goals should be:

- ➢ *S*pecific
- ➢ *M*easurable
- ➢ *A*chievable
- ➢ *R*esults-focused
- ➢ *T*imebound

For example, you might set a goal to earn $200,000 (specific, measurable and results-focused) in 2019 (timebound). If your earnings in 2018 were $150,000, your goal certainly meets the achievable requirement as well, making this a good (S.M.A.R.T.) goal.

While S.M.A.R.T. goals are safe and expected, there's something to be said for dreaming big, too. Try setting at least one goal in each of these areas, and don't be afraid to take your initial goal and multiply it by 10.

Breaking it Down: Your Year at a Glance

Now that you know what your goals are, it's time to break them down into manageable chunks. It's much easier to think about adding 100 people to your mailing list this week than it is to consider the monumental task of adding 5,000 people this year. Use the table below to break your big goals into smaller pieces that you can more easily handle.

YEARLY GOAL	MONTHLY GOAL	WEEKLY GOAL

DAY 17

CASH FLOW LEVERAGING

L everaging the cash flow of your business is important for you as an owner and for potential investors as partners.

One of the first reports with which a business owner should become familiar is the income statement. It shows your revenues, expenses, and profit for a particular period — a snapshot that shows whether or not your business is profitable. A simple equation to remember: Revenue minus Expenses equals Profit/ Loss. It is a good rule of thumb to maintain a monthly report and compile the report each quarter to get a good view of how your cash flow is leveraging. When this information is compiled each quarter, it makes it simpler for you to develop a cash-flow projection for the future. The cash-flow projection shows how cash is expected to flow in and out of your business. It is an important tool for cash-flow management, because it lets you know when your expenditures are too high or whether you might need a short-term investment to deal with a cash-flow surplus.

Below is an income statement template for the first quarter for a service-based business. Not all of the categories in this income statement will apply to your business. Eliminate those that do not apply and add categories where necessary to adapt this template to your business.

Company Name Income Statement for the 1st quarter of (year)				
	Jan	Feb	Mar	Total
REVENUE				
Sales				
Cost of Goods Sold				
Opening Inventory				
Purchases				
Freight				
Minus Closing Inventory				
Total Cost of Goods Sold				
Gross Profit				

EXPENSES

Materials	
Equipment Rentals	
Salary (Owner)	
Wages	
Pension Expense	
Workmen's Compensation Expense	
Total Direct Costs	
General and Administration (G&A)	
Accounting and Legal Fees	
Advertising and Promotion	
Insurance	
Interest	
Office Rent	
Telephone	

Utilities	
Credit Card Charges	
Total G&A	
TOTAL EXPENSES	
NET INCOME BEFORE INCOME TAXES	
INCOME TAXES	
NET INCOME	

Luke 14:28-30

"But don't begin until you count the cost. For who would begin construction of a building without first calculating the cost to see if there is enough money to finish it? Otherwise, you might complete only the foundation before running out of money, and then everyone would laugh at you. They would say, 'There's the person who started that building and couldn't afford to finish it!'"

Take some time to set up your cash-flow spreadsheet, using the example above as a guideline.

_____

_____

_____

_____

_____

_____

_____

_____

_____

_____

_____

LEVERAGING YOUR BUISNESS FOR SUCCESS

You started your business with a vision in mind. You probably daydreamed about what it would look like as you sat in your day-job office waiting for the clock to tell you it was finally time to go home. Maybe, as you scraped ice off your car in preparation for yet another freezing commute in bumper-to-bumper traffic, you fantasized about how it would be to work from home.

What did it look like, this dream business of yours? How did your ideal days roll out? Where did you spend your down time?

Chances are your vision has changed, but you very likely still have a dream of what you want your business — and your life — to look like.

Spend a few minutes to write out (in as much detail as you can) your short- and long-term business and life vision.

1 year:

_____

_____

_____

5 years:

_____

_____

_____

10 *years:*

_____

_____

_____

Create DoAble Tasks

Reaching your goals won't just happen. You have to put in the work in order to achieve new heights.

You've already broken your goals down into monthly and weekly milestones, so now it's time to plan the tasks to reach those milestones. For example, if you set a goal of adding 100 people to your mailing list each week, and you know that your ***website*** landing page converts at 20 percent, then you need to drive 500 new people to your page. You might do that by running paid Facebook ads, sharing your URL on Twitter and LinkedIn, or buying solo ads. (In each case, you'll need to test and track to ensure you're spending and sharing in the correct numbers to reach your goal.)

WEEKLY GOAL	TASK TO ACHIEVE	TASK TO ACHIEVE

ENTREPRENEURSHIP BRANDING

B
randing is often seen as unnecessary by those who do not understand the importance of their business image. It's often overlooked because it's difficult to see the tangible benefits. Without a brand strategy for your business, however, you convey an attitude that "anything goes" … and even for the small business, this can be dangerous. Without a brand, the business lacks a clearly identified purpose. And without a purpose, a business can't stand out from the competition. Branding will direct people to your business purpose.

I will admit that developing a brand strategy can be one of the most difficult and challenging steps in the marketing-plan process, especially when you don't understand the business of marketing. In fact, the development of a brand strategy is the biggest challenge for *most* businesses, but it's a vital step in creating company identity. *Your brand will be communicated in every facet of your business with frequency and consistency.* Therefore, it is important to spend some time developing the right look for your brand because this will be the "face" of your business.

Your brand strategy identifies ***four core components*** of your business … components that can then be used as a blueprint for developing your marketing strategy and tactics. These four core components include:

Purpose: Your business must have a functional and intentional purpose. What is the primary purpose of your business? You need to know this to build a brand.

Consistency: Without consistency, a business will struggle to survive. Nobody will follow inconsistencies with a business. Don't try to overdo your brand. You don't want to confuse your audience as to what your business is all about.

Expression: Understanding the expression of your brand is what helps customers connect with you. Brand expression is just like the personality of a human being … it is made up of the personal qualities we associate with a particular business. Every element of the brand identity, including the color of the logo and the typography of the company name, adds to the personality.

Quality: Perceived quality is also a brand association, though because of its significance, it is accorded a distinct status in the realm of brand equity. Perceived quality is the customer's perception of the overall quality of a brand.

To begin the development of your brand's strategy, you must understand these ***four marketing components***:

o   Primary Target Customer and/or Client

o   Competition

o   Product and Service

o   Unique Selling Proposition

By identifying these components of your marketing plan, you have the basis for developing your brand strategy. An effective branding process creates a unique identity that helps you to stand out from the competition. The power of your brand relies on the ability to remain focused and consistent. That is why defining your target market will help to strengthen your brand's effectiveness.

Colossians 3:17

And whatever you do, in word or deed, do everything in the name of the Lord Jesus, giving thanks to God the Father through him.

Take some time to create your logo and write down your branding ideas.

_____

_____

_____

_____

_____

_____

_____

_____

_____

_____

_____

_____

_____

_____

_____

MASTER MARKETING

Have you ever noticed a business succeeding without marketing? Part of operating a successful business involves understanding the importance of marketing. I have seen businesses close because of the lack of proper marketing; books go unsold because of the lack of proper marketing; movies and music suffer from low sales because of the lack of proper marketing.

If you want to produce wealth, you must include the investment of marketing. Oftentimes, we are reluctant to invest money into areas we don't understand. Know that marketing is an area that every entrepreneur must budget into expenses in order to have a successful business. The fundamental goals of marketing are increasing sales and achieving a sustainable competitive advantage.

Let's talk about some marketing tools you can use. Some are free. Some may cost, but they will offer a great return on your investment.

1. Social Media

Social media is a highly effective marketing tool. Some businesses have been built solely from the utilization of social media. Granted, some negative aspects of social media have come to light in recent years, which is why some people have refrained from it. However, I have learned that social media can be your best friend as well as your worst nightmare (depending on how you use it). You can build considerable business momentum through social media. It is not as difficult as it may seem; many tutorials exist to show you how to utilize this platform to build your audience. You will find advertising via social media to be easier and easier over time.

If you have the money in your budget, you can consider hiring a social media manager. If not, it is easy enough for you to post your products as well as any information that might help your audience learn more about you, your business, and the industry that you're in.

2. Video tutorials

One of the most effective ways to get the word out on your business is to create video tutorials. You can literally build your business without ever leaving your home. If you have a passion for teaching something you have mastered, you have the ability to package your curriculum and teach right from your home through video tutorials. It is also a form of marketing – you are engaging with your audience concerning your business.

Today, YouTube is the second largest search engine in the world behind Google. Whenever someone wants to learn something visually, they head there. You've likely done it yourself countless times. This is a major marketing tool that can be utilized for free. My granddaughter is thrilled by a little boy named Ryan, who does nothing but play with his toys on YouTube. This young man has become wealthy … just by giving "Ryan's Toy Reviews" on You-Tube! Now, he has a toy line in every major store. It just goes to show how important it is to master marketing for business success.

3. A Blog

If you don't have a blog (web log) for your business, then you need to start one immediately. Blogging is marketing. If you want to build an audience for your business, start blogging and asking people questions about the products or services you plan to sell. You will be amazed at the interaction you will have with people simply by talking to them about your business and what you offer.

You want to blog on a site that is built specifically for your business, not on your personal pages. You want to educate people about your business and market its mission and purpose. Partner with people who have a large following so that you can advertise your blog site on their social-media platforms and websites. This will help increase your audience.

Blogging can be tricky if you don't spend time with it. When you blog, ensure that you do so effectively. Don't post thin content. Think about adding value. Give people so much value that you instantly become an authority in their eyes. You must be diligent and disciplined in maintaining your blog; if you are too busy, assign someone from your team to oversee the blogging efforts. You don't want to blog information and leave it cold for weeks afterward. It is important that you remain connected to your audience to build trust.

LinkedIn's publishing platform is a good place to build an audience for your business — and your blog. This is a domain on which anyone can post. You can command a massive audience, giving you instant and immediate reach. This is one of the most powerful strategies you can use to market any business.

4. Facebook ads

One of the most powerful methods you can use to market just about anything these days is Facebook ads. With Facebook, you can reach a specific audience, and you can do it very easily. You can target your audience by interest, age, relationships status, geographic location, and so much more. If you don't know how to utilize Facebook ads, I encourage you to review the tutorials on Facebook and become familiar with promoting ads and adding pixels to your account. This feature does cost; however, you will be amazed how much it will increase your audience.

5. LinkedIn

Do you have a video on your LinkedIn profile? Did you know that you can easily add one? Why not take the time to introduce yourself and your business? Link that to your profile description. This is an easy way to passively market your business, and when it's done right, it can lead to amazing results.

If you have a lot of connections on LinkedIn but you're not posting anything there, begin immediately. You can reach a large audience, especially when your posts go viral. This is a great place to convey the entrepreneurial journey. Talk about your challenges and tell stories. The more effective your stories, the larger your potential reach when you go viral.

You can also reach out to other businesses and collaborate with like-minded entrepreneurs on LinkedIn. It's a great go-to resource for all things business. Too many people overlook this.

6. Email Marketing

Part of any good sales funnel is going to be an email marketing sequence. These are the automated messages that go out to users once they subscribe to your list. Use your email to build a relationship with the subscriber. You can set up a subscriber link on your business website, on your social media platforms, and through Google Analytics. You can also purchase plans through email marketing brands such as Constant Contact, which give you the ability to set up landing pages and email templates to help you build your business.

You never really know what method is going to be the most effective until you pull the trigger and test it out. This will help you better understand what your audience responds to. As a result, you will be a better communicator, better able to sell to your customers.

Proverbs 22:29

Do you see a man skillful and experienced in his work?
He will stand [in honor] before kings;
He will not stand before obscure men.

Plan your marketing ideas and budget.

_____

_____

_____

_____

_____

_____

_____

_____

_____

_____

_____

_____

_____

HOW TO ENLARGE YOUR TERRITORY

The owner of any great company should be looking for ways to expand his or her reach to a larger territory. It's great that you are known on a local level for your business, but with today's technology, you can do business in Japan, China, Virgin Islands, Africa ... all over the world. You should consider going beyond your local area to take your business to greater heights. Yes, your local support is great, and it's necessary as a launching pad. But you should want to soar at some point! Expansion of your territory should be considered as a future endeavor. After you have established your business flow and your current market, after you have established yourself in meeting your customers' needs, you should want to enlarge your territory. Here are a few ideas for approaching this undertaking.

1. Target Your Territory

Determine who you want to target and in what order. Look at your leads, prospects and opportunities to determine possible clientele. Look for areas with "big fish" opportunities. (Don't be afraid to branch outside your local comfort zone; at the same time, make sure you are reaching for attainable projects.)

When you have identified areas into which you'd like to expand, do your research. Check the market in those areas for the products and/or services you plan to provide. It is always important for you to research the demographics, and the need, for what you are offering. If they align with your offering, make sure you prioritize them accordingly.

2. Locate and Connect with Potential Partners

Next, make sure you research the people associated with establishments in the area that are most likely to benefit from what you are selling. Who are the decision makers, the influencers, the champions? Take the time to document this information in the form of buyer contact. Your potential partners may own or operate stores, libraries, boutiques or other entities at which they will be able to promote or sell what you have to offer. The more you know about your prospects, the more effectively you will be able to reach out and communicate with them by phone or email.

3. Develop a Communication Plan with Targeted Potential Partners

Use the information you gathered to communicate with a potential buyer. Develop email messaging that speaks not just to the company, but to the needs of the individual contact. Write short, personalized email messages and phone scripts. Tailored messaging elicits higher callback rates, helping you get to your destination faster.

4. Stay Persistent

Don't stop the process just because it doesn't appear to be working in the first few months. Remember — you represent a new company, and you will need to build trust across the globe. Your persistence will pay off later. Utilize email blasts and automatic phone-call techniques to remain connected to your potential clients. You should be prepared to make between 10 and 15 attempts to contact a potential client before reaching that client. That may be the only connection needed to expand your business. When you get that one potential partner in another state or county, you have now enlarged your territory. It only takes one!

5. Schedule and Execute Your Strategy

Once you have a territory management strategy, use it. Schedule regular meetings – whether face-to-face, phone, email, FaceTime, or Skype — with whoever you have partnered with to sell your products or services. Honor these appointments. Be diligent. Keep all promises made, especially when it comes to the provision of products and services in your new territory.

1 Chronicles 4:10 (NAS)

Now Jabez called on the God of Israel, saying, "Oh that You would bless me indeed and enlarge my border, and that Your hand might be with me, and that You would keep me from harm that it may not pain me!" And God granted him what he requested.

Take some time to write down the territories into which you would like to expand, and why you believe your business would be a good fit for these areas.

_____

_____

_____

_____

_____

_____

_____

_____

_____

_____

_____

_____

PROFIT

Profit is not the legitimate purpose of business.
The legitimate purpose of business is to provide a
product or service that people need and do it so well that it's profitable.
— James Rouse

THINK LIKE A BOSS

Congratulations on starting your business! You must now think like a Boss. Your business will succeed only if you put the work into it. Many people want to be the Boss ... that is, until they are faced with the prospect of running their own business. Thinking like a Boss with your own business is a much greater responsibility than being a Boss within someone else's company. Everything about your business will be *your* responsibility to produce.

"Boss" is simply another term I use for "entrepreneur." As defined on various websites, an entrepreneur *is a person who organizes and operates a business or businesses, taking on greater than normal financial risks to do so.* Your business is a financial risk. Most importantly, it represents your time and integrity.

Therefore, you must think differently now. Your thinking is a direct reflection of your business. If you have a poor mentality, such as low self-esteem, you will think and operate with that poor mentality within your business. You must think like a BOSS! You must be ahead of the game, always forecasting, always preparing for the best and the worst. Bosses are people with Vision, Confidence, Leadership and Persistence ... and they are Competitive. Bosses take ownership and responsibility. They know that if their business is going to succeed, they must take pride in what they started.

Bosses value their time. You *must* understand the importance and the value of your time as a Boss. Don't allow your time to be hijacked or monopolized by unplanned situations. You must keep an organized schedule. Not only is it of vital importance that you value *your* time; it's equally as important to value *others'* time. Optimum time management is a major responsibility you must cultivate as a Boss.

Bosses surround themselves with a strong team. It is imperative for you to build relationships beyond your status. If your circle consists only of people who work for you or are led by you, then you have a small circle. A Boss is always looking to connect with those who are smarter, wiser, and have succeeded in the areas they hope to reach. A Boss is never afraid of connecting with others whose businesses are more successful than theirs.

When you think like a Boss, you are prepared to hustle. I like to think of a Boss as a grand hustler who is not afraid to take risks to Level Up to that next business or expand around the globe. Hustler decisions are made in the boardroom by, and with, people who know how to think like a Boss. You have to change your mentality from that of a mailroom worker. Not that there's anything wrong with the guy who's delivering the mail to office personnel … but a Boss would aspire to own a mail service and contract with various offices to deliver their mail! How do you think Federal Express and United Parcel Service (also known as FedEx and UPS) and other shipping services originated? Someone began to think like a Boss and decided to implement a plan that eventually brought in billions of dollars. You can be that same type of Boss when you learn how to *think* like a Boss!

Bosses look beyond being employees. They focus on being *owners*. Here are a few pointers to help you to start your journey to Thinking Like a Boss:

1. ***Embrace the thought of Being a Boss*** — Working is not the issue. Doing what you love and are passionate about is the issue. When you are ready to pursue your passion, making the decision to embrace it is necessary to becoming a Boss. *"Your work is going to fill a large part of your life, and the only way to be truly satisfied is to do what you believe is great work. And the only way to do great work is to love what you do."* — **Steve Jobs**

2. ***Know why you want to be a Boss*** — Don't just desire to be a Boss because somebody else is doing it. Have the right motive for being a Boss. Thinking like a Boss requires you to have the right motive. Your heart must really be into building your business. There will be some rough times starting off, so you want to make sure your motive was fueled with the right passion. Otherwise you will quit long before you begin to see a profit.

3. ***Stop Dreaming about it and Do it*** — Many people dream about being a Boss, but allow fear to prevent them from making any moves toward Bosshood. Step out of that comfort zone. You will never become a Boss if you're afraid to step out of your familiar territory. Bosses take risks!

4. ***Training is Essential to your Growth*** – You may know *exactly* how to start your business. You may know *exactly* what type of service or product you will provide. Nonetheless, it is always a good rule of thumb for a Boss to gain more education about his or her craft. Never stop Leveling Up. You

may consider yourself an expert in the field into which your business will fall. But there is always someone else who has more knowledge than you and can help take your business to the next level.

5. ***Dress Like a Boss*** — You must understand that your business reflects *you*. How you dress is an indication of how your business operates. When you *think* like a Boss, you understand the importance of *looking* like a Boss. Always be prepared to walk into the boardroom and deliver a pitch in style. You can do this on a budget and still look like a Boss. Never take for granted that because you are the Boss it doesn't matter. Your clients and potential partners are watching you!

6. ***Remain Mentally, Emotionally and Physically Healthy*** — Connect with those who will encourage you to take care of yourself along the way. Being the Boss is not easy. You will need to remain encouraged as you take this journey. Make sure you maintain a habit that will keep you mentally, emotionally and physically healthy. This can include journaling, reading, horseback riding, exercising, hiking — whatever you must do to release stress and keep up with the demands of being the Boss!

Proverbs 10:4

Poor is he who works with a negligent and idle hand,
But the hand of the diligent makes him rich.

Why do you think you are a Boss and not an Employee? Write down some reasons.

_____

_____

_____

_____

_____

_____

_____

_____

_____

_____

_____

_____

_____

_____

MASTER COMMUNICATOR/PUBLIC SPEAKING

You may have heard the cliché, "Communication is key." This is true in any relationship, whether personal or business. One of the most important areas a business owner should want to master is communication with potential clients, customers and team members. In order to communicate, one needs to understand the elements of communication and how to pull them off. Here are the things you must do when communicating with others about your business.

First, you must have a precise and well-thought-out pitch stating the *purpose* of your business. If you were given 10 minutes to sell your business to a board of directors for a loan to fund it, you must be prepared to present your information thoroughly.

Second, you must exhibit *confidence*. Confidence is essential in successful communication. Public speaking can be intimidating when you are not prepared or even sure about what you are presenting. It is quite noticeable when someone lacks confidence in what they are peddling.

Third, you must *pace* yourself when presenting information to your audience in order to give them the opportunity to process what is being presented. Never rush your material to get your point across. A hasty presentation shows a lack of confidence in and uncertainty of the product or service you are providing. Give time for your audience to hear your pitch and give them an opportunity to ask questions.

Fourth, you must be sure to *engage* with your audiences. Make eye contact with everyone in the room. Never look down or use "uh" and "um" as sentence fillers. This goes back to a lack of confidence — people can tell if you are scattered in your thoughts and not prepared to present the information you are sharing.

Fifth, be sure to *remember* your customer's, team member's or business partner's name. People will connect with you when they see that you care enough to call them by name when you are communicating with them. As a master communicator, you must listen as much as you communicate.

Becoming a master communicator is a major undertaking. Listen, learn and evolve. Become a master of your voice and as you grow, your style of communication will grow, too. Here are a few pointers to think about as you develop your communication skills.

1. Your words

It's been said that people judge you by the words you use, and this is true. Choose your words wisely. They have the power to move nations ... and they have the power to destroy as well. When you speak, use your words carefully. Do not assume that familiarity with your team, customers or business partners give you leeway to use unprofessional words.

2. Your vocabulary

An expanded vocabulary will set you apart. It enhances the communication process and draws others in. By the way ... expanding your vocabulary does not mean using slang words!

3. Your emotion

Communicating emotion while speaking is vital. The key here is to show emotion without "getting emotional." Emotion can be quite an effective communicator. But it is imperative that you use *positive* emotions. You can lose good team members and clientele by displaying negative/unhealthy ones.

4. Your enunciation

Proper enunciation is an often-overlooked key to effective communication. It can make or break your business deal. People need to understand you, so you must make sure that they do. Clear enunciation gives a little "punch" to your communication.

5. Your speaking position

When you're communicating, especially in a presentation situation, your speaking position — whether you are standing, sitting or kneeling — can communicate a lot. Make sure you are standing or sitting in the right area when speaking or presenting. When you enter a room for a meeting, always allow the host to tell you where to sit; never assume you are to sit at the head of the table unless you are in your own meeting and space.

Proverbs 15:2

The tongue of the wise commends knowledge, but the mouths of fools pour out folly.

Write down some ways to improve your communication skills.

BUSINESS INTEGRITY

Integrity is one of the most important qualities of great leadership in business. Businesses that have lasted for years are still around today because of the integrity of those who operate them. These people know that integrity is one of the foundations of business.

Integrity involves doing the right thing because it is the right thing to do. It involves adhering to strong moral principles. Honesty is a strong component. And that's what helps ensure the success of a business. Great bosses and leaders are honest with customers and partners. They give promises carefully, sometimes even reluctantly — but once they have made those promises, they follow through on them without fail.

You must be very careful, as a business owner, not to exhibit a lack of integrity. Being honest with your customers, team and partners will take your business a long way. If you start out being honest, you won't have to scramble later to make up for being dishonest.

When you are late for a meeting with an investor or are late getting your committed business plan to that investor, you lose integrity and are therefore subject to lose out on business funding. When your customer feels you did not meet your product's quality commitment, your company loses integrity. When you find that a company mistake keeps you from delivering a service, you lose integrity ... unless you not only apologize, but include in your apology the *actual reason* you can't deliver.

Building a successful business takes time; it takes blood, sweat and tears; and it takes a heck of a lot of hard work. People who operate businesses with integrity already realize that there are no short-cuts. They don't look for ways to cheat their customers and clients to make more money, because they already know that ultimately, they're cheating themselves. In order to succeed as an entrepreneur, you must demonstrate integrity at all times.

Proverbs 11:1

A false balance and dishonest business practices are extremely offensive to the LORD, But an accurate scale is His delight.

Write down ways you plan to implement integrity in your business.

_____

_____

_____

_____

_____

_____

_____

_____

_____

_____

_____

_____

_____

_____

Resources for Your business

No business — or life — operates in a vacuum. You need help. People, tools and training are all critical to your success. Some examples of necessary resources include:

Business Tools

- Web hosting
- Mailing list management
- Social media presence
- Landing page creation
- Webinar hosting

Business Training

- Email marketing
- Facebook ads
- Blogging/content marketing
- Technology training

People

- Virtual assistants
- Copywriters
- Graphic designers

- Video/audio editors

When you think of your goals and vision for the coming year, make a note about the resources needed to accomplish those goals. Some of them you likely already have; some you will need to research and add to your current list.

What's missing from my business and life that will help me achieve my goals?

_____

_____

_____

_____

_____

Accountability AND Support

Aside from the tools and training you'll need to achieve your goals, you'll very likely need support and accountability from others as well.

Who will keep you motivated when you just want to give up?

Who will help increase conversions on your landing pages?

Who will share different ideas and perspectives with you to help increase sales?

As a small-business owner, you need a solid human support system to help you get the right things done. These support people will include:

- ➤ Your spouse or significant other
- ➤ Your business partner (if you have one)
- ➤ Your mastermind groups
- ➤ Your accountability partners
- ➤ Your business and/or life coach

Ecclesiastes 7:1a

A good name is better than precious ointment; ...

Which of these human assets do you currently have? Which do you need? What roles will they fill in your goal setting and business growth?

PERSON	ROLE

MASTERING YOUR TIME

Your time is your most valuable resource as an entrepreneur. When you're in business for yourself, time is as precious a commodity as money. You can't afford to waste time due to poor time management. Improper assessment of your daily time can lead to poor performance, frustration, bad customer service and a decline in mobility. Entrepreneurship can be very demanding, especially when you have a busy personal life as well, so taking care to manage your work-life balance is critical.

Granted, there comes a point in everyone's life when there just doesn't seem to be enough time to do everything. It can often be difficult — and very frustrating — to find enough hours in the day to accomplish tasks.

Managing your time is all about mastering your schedule. Making time work for you helps you to build a successful business. ***Lack of preparation*** can cause you to lose sight of your plan for the day, week, month or year. As mentioned earlier, proper planning is most important for success ... especially when it comes to scheduling appointments, meetings, deadline dates, work assignments, etc. You must get control of your day-to-day operation by maximizing your time. I can't stress it enough: *You can't afford to allow your time to go by day after day without proper time management.*

Take 30 minutes at the start of each day to plan that day. Rank everything by importance; that way, if something unexpected comes up, you'll know what you can postpone. Successful businesspeople always jump on the most important thing first. What's the most important thing you should do right now? Learning to answer that question quickly, then acting on it, will increase your productivity tenfold.

There are many ways to misuse your time in the course of a day. As an entrepreneur, you have to be careful not to allow *distractions* to interrupt your flow. Distractions come in all shapes and sizes. It could be something as simple as lacking a specific, private work space, which means you're putting up with noise or other people.

Not only can you mishandle your time with distractions; you can also mishandle your time via *procrastination*. Everyone, at some point, has given in to procrastination … which is fed by such issues as failure to prioritize, indecisiveness, fear, avoidance and confusion. But habitual procrastination can result in *nothing getting done*, day after day. This is not good for a successful entrepreneur. It can cause many issues for you down the line. Don't allow procrastination to destroy your time management and stymie the growth of your business.

It is also important to make sure you get the proper rest. Your body and mind aren't designed to sit and work for hours without any stimulation. Take a break! When you're planning your day, schedule some time to break away from your work. If you don't, you'll lose creativity and become mentally stagnant. Your performance will eventually decline.

Here are a few tips to help you develop good time-management skills as an entrepreneur.

1. ***Review your to-do list.*** This list should be prepared weekly and reviewed daily.

2. ***Prioritize.*** Make it a daily or weekly task to prioritize each day.

3. ***Delegate.*** This is important for your schedule to flow right for the day. Make sure you delegate assignments that need not be on your to-do list for the day or week. This is also an opportunity to review assignments that have been delegated in the past.

4. ***Complete the most important tasks first.*** When you prioritize, it's easier to monitor what's most important and work from your list accordingly.

5. ***Block off time for difficult situations.*** During your day, there needs to be time allotted to handling matters you may not have previously considered. Mark these as high-priority tasks.

6. ***Schedule.*** Allot time for handling things (emails, phone calls, etc.) that may not be the highest priority, but important, nonetheless.

7. ***Plan ahead.*** Take some time to sit down for a moment to think about the things that need to be addressed in the future. Always stay ahead of your current schedule.

8. ***Break/Rest.*** One of the most important things to do is schedule time to rest and reflect on something that is calming. This will increase your creativity and thought processes. Take this time to read, listen to music or enjoy a podcast.

Ecclesiastes 3:1

For everything there is a season, a time for every activity under heaven.

Create a schedule for your daily, weekly and monthly tasks.

_____

_____

_____

_____

_____

_____

_____

_____

_____

_____

_____

_____

_____

_____

_____

_____

_____

PLANNING FOR THE FUTURE

Ask any business owner the secret to a better business, and they'll tell you it's focus. To allow yourself to be distracted by other opportunities or ideas is to dilute the power of your core business.

While this can be true in many cases, it can also cause you, as a purpose-seeking entrepreneur to freeze in your tracks, unwilling to move in *any* direction for fear of choosing the wrong one. Much like the college graduate who feels trapped in a job simply because that's what he or she knows, you'll only end up hating your business and wishing for a day job again.

Rather than wearing blinders to keep you laser-focused every moment, however, take some time to explore other possibilities. Look for complementary ideas that are a natural match for one another. For example, one prolific and in-demand jewelry designer turned years of teaching and a passion for jewelry into a wildly popular training program for up-and-coming designers. Now she divides her time between creating stunning engagement rings and teaching others how to have a business they love. Had she remained focused only on jewelry design, she would still be popular, and still doing what she loves, but the addition of the training course allowed her to find her true passion. Don't be afraid to follow that winding path from time to time. You never know what you might discover around the next bend.

Exercise: Below, create a list of the new experiences you'd like to have. Then, create a list of future projects. Productivity gurus refer to the latter a "someday" list. It's a list of the projects and plans you want to do, but *not right now.* Much like your New Experiences list, the Someday List is a living document on which you'll record every new project that crosses your mind. Some will be good. Most will not. But that's okay. The point is to not close your mind to the possibilities.

NEW EXPERIENCES I WANT TO HAVE	
	My Plan: Date Completed:
	My Plan: Date Completed:
	My Plan: Date Completed:
	My Plan: Date Completed:
	My Plan: Date Completed:
	My Plan: Date Completed:
	My Plan: Date Completed:

MY SOMEDAY LIST

Day 28

INVESTING SMART

It is vital that entrepreneurs develop additional revenue streams and create wealth outside of their businesses to ensure their financial security. This process can be viewed as a short-term investment and a long-term investment.

The most important factor to understand is how to build a diversified investment portfolio. There are many ways to invest — mutual funds, savings, whole-life insurance, Individual Retirement Accounts (IRAs), 401K plans, stocks and bonds. That's why the most important investment you can make as an entrepreneur is an investment in a financial advisor who can assist you with all your investment plans. I personally invested in a financial advisor to help me develop a comprehensive investment portfolio.

A type of investment that I advocate is buying real-estate property, accumulating it alone or through partnering with other real-estate investors. I discussed my successful entry into the world of real estate — purchasing homes with cash, then renting them out — earlier in the book. One of the reasons I prefer real estate is the quick return on my investment. Overall, real estate can be an incredible investment opportunity. It carries certain risks, but it allows entrepreneurs to leverage more money via mortgages, add considerable value as owners and potentially benefit from stable passive income.

While real estate can be a great area in which to invest, there are a number of things beginners should be aware of to avoid simple mistakes and hedge potential risks. Do your homework in order to invest smart. If you decide to invest in real estate, make sure you connect with people who are familiar with the logistics of real estate and the demographics of the areas in which you are interested in purchasing properties. People in real estate are usually friendly and willing to help those starting out, so just reach out to active real estate investors in your area.

Once you have a mentor, you will need to find a strong Realtor and broker. These people will help you find quality properties and enable you to execute deals promptly. People will always need houses and offices. It's for that reason that, in my opinion, real estate will always be a smart investment for entrepreneurs.

Matthew 25:14-17

" ... The Kingdom of Heaven can be illustrated by the story of a man going on a long trip. He called together his servants and entrusted his money to them while he was gone. He gave five bags of silver to one, two bags of silver to another, and one bag of silver to the last— dividing it in proportion to their abilities. He then left on his trip. The servant who received the five bags of silver began to invest the money and earned five more. The servant with two bags of silver also went to work and earned two more ... "

What you see your investment portfolio looking like? Write your vision.

_____

_____

_____

_____

_____

_____

_____

_____

_____

_____

_____

DAY 29

CREATING A LEGACY

As a successful entrepreneur, you've learned many valuable lessons. You've had a number of successes and plenty of failures from which others can learn. Why not share what you have learned and educate future generations? Entrepreneurship goes beyond mere business. It has more to do with building a legacy than anything else. There have been all too many cases in which founders of successful businesses passed away ... and the businesses they spent decades building died with them.

A *legacy* is defined as "anything handed down from the past, as from an ancestor or predecessor," according to Dictionary.com. Each of us has the power to create a legacy. In fact, we make our legacies every day — whether we think about it or not. Even if we *do* think about our legacies, we don't completely control them. Legacies live in the minds of those who know us — or in the ideas and values we leave behind. Do you believe in leaving your children a sizable inheritance? That's all well and good, but what's so wrong with utilizing your success as a launch pad for your child's successful entrepreneurial endeavors?

In the late 19th century, there were two very wealthy families: the Vanderbilts and the Rockefellers. Soon after the Vanderbilt family patriarch passed away, the family fortune was quickly depleted, leaving many heirs completely broke. On the other hand, the

Rockefeller fortune is still going strong today, six generations later. I believe the Rockefellers' fortune continued from generation to generation because they established a strategic process for not only creating a legacy but transferring wealth.

If you want your family to be successful in carrying your legacy or business long after you are gone, you need to consider the strategic approach of passing the torch to your family members while you are alive. This approach must be woven into the fabric of your business, benefiting your children and your children's children. There is an old saying that if you give a man a fish, you will feed him for a day, but if you teach a man to fish, you will feed him for a lifetime. I totally agree with this. Great businesspeople have left great inheritances for offspring who lacked a sense of direction to continue the company's success because they were not woven into the fabric of the business.

I am not saying your children must desire to do what you have created as a business, but I am saying it is important for them to understand your business and vision if you want it to become a legacy for your family and if you want your family to feast on the fruits of your labor for generations. It's OK to leave your family money, but if they don't know how to handle it or operate a business, they will run through what you have taken years to build. This is what happened to the Vanderbilts. This family had billions of dollars, but the wealth did not last.

It's not hard for your family to learn how to *spend* money. For anyone who wants to have nice things and enjoy life, spending is an inevitable pursuit. However, the ability to learn how to build wealth and prepare for future generations will need to be *taught* as a legacy for your family.

I realize that this subject may have been the furthest thing from your mind if you're just starting out in business and have yet to even make your first dollar. But if you plan to be successful in business, one of the most important things you can do is look beyond where you are now and think of your posterity. Your business success will one day be a legacy for them. Again, many companies have continued to thrive, long after the founder's transitioning from this world, because that founder applied strategies not only for *building* wealth but leaving a *legacy* of wealth.

You need to consider what your family will remember about you. I wouldn't want to just reap the benefits of my success myself. My desire would be to build a business with my children, family and community in mind. My desire would be that my business would still be thriving, and others would still be reaping the benefits from it, long after I am gone.

Proverbs 13:22 (AMP}

A good man leaves an inheritance to his children's children,
And the wealth of the sinner is stored up for [the hands of] the righteous.

Write down ways you would create a business legacy to leave for your family.

_____

_____

_____

_____

_____

_____

_____

_____

_____

_____

_____

_____

_____

_____

EMBRACING THE WEALTHY LIFE

Most entrepreneurs don't become successful overnight. They make up their minds to choose that path to wealth. The path to becoming wealthy is about changing your mindset and believing. Wealth creates, or increases, a positive impact on your loved ones, your community and your life. Wealth enables you to enjoy confidence about day-to-day living ... now and into your future. Wealth gives you a sense of security, not just personal security but security for your family's sake.

The best way to achieve any definition of wealth is to understand your goals and prepare a plan to achieve them. The earlier you begin your journey to wealth, the more likely you are to succeed. Building wealth is not just about you; it's also about those who are connected to you. We're as successful as we deserve to be; the amount of work we've put in determines the amount of success we've achieved. Success is something that has to be earned. Wherever we are right now in life is where we deserve to be. We've done what's necessary to be where we are at this very moment. Yes, it can be scary at times. We have all had that fear of what happens when we achieve our biggest life goals ... fulfill a dream ... experience a higher level of success.

You may be working so hard to get to where you want to be, you haven't even thought of what it will be like once you begin to see success in your entrepreneurial journey. No worries. You belong there! When you put in the work to live a life of wealth, it is OK to embrace it. You are now ready to celebrate what you have achieved. Own it as the entrepreneur you really were created to be. Keep walking toward your wealthy place. Don't give up; you are headed in the right direction. I will see you there!

Proverbs 10:22

The blessing of the LORD brings [true] riches,
And He adds no sorrow to it [for it comes as a blessing from God].

Describe, in writing, the ways you plan to embrace your wealthy place.

_____

_____

_____

_____

_____

_____

_____

_____

_____

_____

_____

_____

_____

_____

_____

_____

ABOUT THE BOOK

This book will challenge you to turn your hobby, skill, interest and/or passion into profit! Tiffany describes practical and spiritual strategies to pursue your passion to become a successful entrepreneur. This guide will outline basic foundations of starting your business and leveraging it for success. You will learn how to prepare a step-by-step, detailed business plan you can use to launch your own small business. You will learn how to creatively pursue your passion and build your brand, negotiate deals, partner with others, register your business, create a marketing campaign, develop social media profiles, and sell your product or service for a profit. Whether you are a busy professional, married or single, this book will help you develop a plan for multiple income streams to live the life you desire! This 30-day guide is designed to help you Level Up your passion and build your brand to get wealth by doing what you already love to do!

ABOUT THE AUTHOR

Tiffany Moorer is the chief executive officer of Moorer Enterprises. She is an entrepreneur who has tripled her net worth in less than five years by applying Biblical principles and practical strategies to gain wealth. She has expanded her streams of income through authoring several books and starting her own publishing company, ISpeak Publishing Services LLC. Mrs. Moorer has also added real-estate investing to her portfolio by purchasing several investment properties. Mrs. Moorer is a true **trailblazer** in building wealth and empowering others to pursue their dreams. She is the author of ***I Still Win: A Life of Love, Tragedy & Triumph.*** She is known as a ***game changer*** because she is known for taking a leap of faith in a project and mastering it for continual growth. Her experience in building streams of income has enabled her to coach many others who have increased their net worth by following her coaching techniques. She is a firm believer that God has given each of us the power and ability to produce wealth, according to ***Deuteronomy 8:18.***

Bibliography

Corporations Online Filing System. (n.d.). Retrieved from https://www.ark.org/sos/ofs/docs/index.php

Legacy. (n.d.). Retrieved from https://www.dictionary.com/browse/legacy (n.d.). Retrieved from https://www.dfa.arkansas.gov/income-tax/small-business-corporate-sub-s/

Small Business Administration. (n.d.). Retrieved from https://www.sba.gov/